A Black Voice in the Wilderness

A Black Voice in the Wilderness

From the Okantah Blog

by

Mwatabu S. Okantah

AFRICA WORLD PRESS
TRENTON | LONDON | CAPE TOWN | NAIROBI | ADDIS ABABA | ASMARA | IBADAN | NEW DELHI

AFRICA WORLD PRESS
541 West Ingham Avenue | Suite B
Trenton, New Jersey 08638

Copyright © 2024, Mwatabu S. Okantah

All rights reserved. No part of this publication may be reproduced, stored in a retrieval system or transmitted in any form or by any means electronic, mechanical, photocopying, recording or otherwise without the prior written permission of the publisher.

Book design: LiteBook Prepress Services
Cover Design: Ashraful Haque
Cover Art & Illustrations: Courtesy of Rob Frostbyte King

Cataloging-in-Publication Data may be obtained from the Library of Congress.

ISBNs: 978-1-56902-856-8 (HB)
        978-1-56902-857-5 (PB)

Prologue

"I freed a thousand slaves. I could have freed a thousand more if only they knew they were slaves."

--Harriet Tubman

Dedication

To my wife, Aminah, for being my soul-mate, for being my best friend, for always being there and for being the Sweet Messenger that you have always been.

Contents

Forward ix
Introduction: Through One Poet's Eyes xi

From the Black Poet-Tree — 1

i, too, am a witness 2
hard truths 3
MAGA whiteness 4
at Cracker Barrel 5
colorblind? 6
nostalgia 7
pandemic 8
Babylon America 9
"Demo-Crazy" 10
No! 11
a blue-black on black crime 12
Afreeka 13
what promise? 14
first time i met poetry 15

A Poet's Vision — 17

"Sick and Tired of Being Sick and Tired!" 18
A Critical Race Reckoning 21

Still Strangers	25
Black Sun in the Western Sky	29
When Is Now!	33
The N-Word, or Ashes to Ashes and Dust to Dust	38
The Way Forward	41
Race: The Elephant in the Room	46
Invented Reality: Trump/DeSantis/Republican Insanities	51
Big Lies	55
Epilogue	59
Suggested Reading	60
About the Author	61

Forward

A Black Voice in the Wilderness is a poetic and insightful meditation on not only what it means to be Black in America, but also a reflection on the current violent reverberation of white supremacy in and on American society. Bell Hooks reminds us in her provocative text, *Sisters of the Yam: Black Women and Self-Recovery*, that we need to speak of pain to remember them and that in remembering we must give our anguish words. In essence, we must testify. Throughout *A Black Voice in the Wilderness*, Okantah testifies. From his first rendering in "I, too, am a witness (for James Baldwin)" to "Big Lies" he weaves the African American historical experience into the threads of the present which demonstrates the value, appeal, and timeliness of this work.

Black Americans 'overstand' deferred dreams of racial justice and Black freedom colliding with white supremacy. Okantah describes modern-day white supremacy in "Sick and Tired of Being Sick and Tired!" when he muses that white supremacy has masked itself as "James" rather than "Jim Crow"—inevitably mutating and strengthening into the current right-wing political movement that continues to mobilize against Black lives. Writing that "anti-democratic measures coming out of Republican-dominated state legislatures and recent so-called Supreme Court rulings signal the mocking resurrection of Jim Crow with the same old face but renamed, James," he is noting the increasingly anti-human legislative bills that are racist, transphobic, homophobic and gendered coming out of many states.

Through poetry and prose, *A Black Voice in the Wilderness* reminds us that race and "white rage" continue to be the mechanisms that move against Black lives. Taking up the movement against Critical Race

Theory (CRT) and the Black Lives Matter movement, Okantah contemplates in his piece, "Race: The Elephant in the Room," how Republican states and right-winged movements are attempting to weaponize their "ignorance and arrogance" to "conserve an archaic status quo that was never intended to embrace 21st century American lives."

Yet, despite the anguish Okantah also pens of critical Black hope which he refers to as "black light." For example, he writes that despite "MAGA Donald Trump as President of the United States. Mother Emanual AME Church in Charleston. Charlottesville. George Floyd. Breonna Taylor. A Tree of Life Synagogue in Pittsburgh. Colorado Springs. The Covid 19 pandemic. Tyre Nichols… [I] …hope that the power of my words might bring black light into a white-dark world and help to heal wounded souls." This critical Black hope is weaved in other texts such as Robin Kelly's *Freedom Dreams* and Bell Hooks' *Sisters of the Yam: Black Women and Self-Recovery*. This critical hope is urgent, calling white Americans to step forward and act in urgency and in support of Black Lives.

Dr. Amoaba Gooden, Professor and Vice-President
People, Culture and Belonging
Kent State University
2023

Introduction
Through One Poet's Eyes

Poetry is how I see. I never know when a poem might present itself or when a poem might choose me. I write because I have something to say and I live in an age when I can create my own blog-space to say it. I write to contribute to that deeply deep Black Story Well.

I subscribe to the message in Ayi Kwei Armah's novel, *2000 Seasons*. African people have experienced the descent, 1000 seasons hurtling down deep into slavery. We are now experiencing the steep climb, 1000 seasons crawling maimed from it. We are a people in need of physical, psychological and spiritual healing. Complete recovery and reclamation will not occur in this lifetime, but I believe it will come.

I write because poetry, prose and music are the weapons I have chosen to wield in this struggle, not only to revive the spirit of my people, but for a suffering humanity as well. I write because I believe "word sounds have power!" I began www.theokantahblog.com in response to so many people asking for my opinions on the numerous issues that appear to be dividing a nation that has always been divided; a nation always at war with itself. Big lies, "fake news" and "alternative facts" did not begin with Donald Trump.

This is a nation born in paradox. The Founding Fathers did not really believe that "all men are created equal." A nation that lies to itself can only be a lost nation. Donald Trump's appeal to "Make America Great Again," is the clarion call to return to the good old days when the original Big Lie was transformed into cruel American truth.

Like James Baldwin, I, too, am a witness: MAGA Donald Trump as President of the United States. Mother Emanuel AME Church in Charleston. Charlottesville. George Floyd. Breonna Taylor. A Tree of Life Synagogue in Pittsburgh. Colorado Springs. The Covid 19 pandemic. Tyre Nichols. I write in the moment in the hope the power of my words might bring black light into a white-dark world and help to heal wounded souls.

Mwatabu S. Okantah,
The Muntu Kuntu Energy Poet
2023
www.mkepoet1.com

From the
Black Poet-Tree

i, too, am a witness
(for James Baldwin)

no,
we are not their "Negro"
or their "Nigger"
or their "Black" or their "Minority"
or their "Person of Color"
or whatever they think to call us next—
always something other than
who we have always been
or who we might be
or who we might become.

in this ever-evolving world
truth is rinsed white
while the dispossessed
are expected to forget what we know
to be true
deep in our bones.

we live with anger.
sleep with it.
wake up with it.
carry it around.
pass it up
from one generation to the next
making a way out of no way.

in this world
being conscious and black
(no matter the shade)
is too black
and to love being black
is still considered
dangerous.

hard truths
(for Dan D'Aurelio)

i know he meant well.
he is a good neighbor.
he cares and keeps a watchful eye.
we live in a racially diverse neighborhood.
we exist in vastly different worlds.

he came over with a question about
missionaries,
with a magazine story about a Pastor in Kintampo,
in Ghana,
that needs a new truck.
he wants to help.

in that moment i did not want
to tell him of the troubles
missionaries have wrought throughout
Africa—
sent there
to disguise the real terror of the strange white men
that came and plundered and raped
and colonized all in the name of the white Jesus.

they came with new magic
with Bibles with machines with guns that mesmerized
black minds that terrorized
black bodies as things slowly fell apart—
visitors became
masters,
Africans became subjugated
became impoverished
and left looking to the people they think
look like that picture of Jesus
to save them:

hard truths
invite harder conversations.

MAGA whiteness

white privilege is
"Vanilla ISIS"
reigning down MAGA whiteness
terrorizing the Capitol
with glee.

white privilege is
rabid-dog folks showing up
for the whole world
to see
shouting in the lynch-mob spirit of being white and free.

white privilege is
watching the good folks in shock
pretending they don't
understand what they know
we all see.

white privilege is
white folks
being
deathly afraid of each other
and they know the real reasons why.

white privilege is
even precious blue lives
don't matter
when 45
transmutes objective truth into bogus white lies.

"USA! USA!"

at Cracker Barrel

for many white people
being together
amongst themselves
is the preferred
normal.

they simply find it easier
to render
people
who look "other"
invisible.

blinded by color
they see only bright
whiteness
reflected black
before their eyes.

Buckhorn, PA

colorblind?

watching them watching me
(at a Cracker Barrel no less)
reminds me
us versus them
is real
even when
many of them are so profoundly harmless.

for too many white people
being white
makes it possible
to pretend
to not see
the "darker
brother."

never really color blind
they see skin color
through the lens of their own
comfort zone
sublime
in white-people
time.

Buckhorn, PA

nostalgia

lost in lost causes
the see no evil
hear no evil
people long for a history they proudly imagine
in "golden age" Hollywood movies.

MAGA bully wanna
resurrect ghosts from the *Gone with the Wind* past
him think Melania must be
Vivien Leigh's Scarlet Ohara
and he be Clark Gable's Rhett Butler.

Trump really-really wannabe President
Jeff Davis of the Confederate States of America
so he can wrap him
real Self forever in the Stars and
Bars.

      Trumpworld

pandemic

sitting in my car
outside grocery store
pondering
being a tall dread locked black man
wearing bandana covering
my face
pondering being shot
just trying to pick up some eggs.

pondering.

Ahmaud Arbery
was just
jogging.
they could see
his face.
they bullet-lynched him
2020 Georgia citizen's arrest style
just because they could trap him in their space.

pondering.

viral
white-fears
more deadly than Covid 19
in this deranged
red white blue
Skinner-
    box
    rat race.

Babylon America

Trumpian politrickster murders opponent
in cartoon reel time
then with smug go sour
Gosar straight face
claims no violent intent
him just reaching out
to young people
no apologies necessary
no need:

that Rittenhouse boy
must have heard the call
deeply deep in his whitemare
dreams
him kill two people
wounded another
him claim self-defense
him jury-peers verdict him
justified and free.

"Demo-Crazy"

the mindless flock and
the fake negroes
just keep
drinking Trump Kool-Aid
while the 45
henchmen
mock hallowed
Founding Father illusions:

politricks.

enslaved Africans
had a better grip
on the real in their time.
they knew
"dem dogs make dem
laws
and dem dogs
break dem laws."

no one
had to tell them
what was
what
or who
was who.

No!

tv commercial declared,
"We all have an immigrant story...."

No!

Africans were
kidnapped,
ripped away from villages,
ripped away from
everything they knew,
ripped away from
everyone they
loved,
yet America persists
in stubborn denial of this truth.
slavery was the engine
that made this nation
great—
no 60 second public service spot
can capture this story:

no name
for wandering
refugees
born in this still strange land,
caught in the vise-grip of American glory.

a blue-black on black crime
(for Tyre Nichols)

people don't
have to ask why
we fear
the police
    any
more.

five brazen blue-black brothers
    beat
down
another black mother's Sun
beyond senseless into another same old American
death.

could have been
    one
of them caught
on the wrong side of
their "protect and serve"
blue line.

demented white supremacy in
    black
face.
black self-loathing
showing out in a brute-badge
blue-black on black crime.

Afreeka

i cry for my Africa
i hurt for my Africa
i smile for my Africa
i laugh with my Africa
i feel
i see
i dream
i sing black poetry
for my Africa.

i am
my
Afreeka—

free …

what promise?

King declared
he'd been to the mountain top,
said he'd seen
the Promised Land,
but what promise did
he see?
what land?

another video?
how many more black lives
must go dead?
blue knee on neck of handcuffed George Floyd.
no knock bullets shot through Breonna Taylor's door.
armed police always claim they are afraid
before and after they make war.

afraid of what?
afraid of who?
to disguise the demons
lurking deep inside
the private corners of their nights
fear is the mask
they wear.

is their fear imagined or is it real?
dis-ease or barking dog rage?
how many more injustices will it take?
is justice blind or is she just blindfolded?
or is it just the same old
stark black truth
turned into same old America does not really care?

first time i met poetry

first time i met poetry
it frightened me
into believing lyrical word sounds
possess real power.

discovered that power
was born in me,
could feel it
rumbling up through my voice.

poetry opened my eyes
to see,
tuned my ears
to hear.

poetry empowered me to be—
to become
one more strong branch
growing out of that ancient Black Poet-Tree.

    Ubuntu*
    (Zulu)

---

* A quality that includes the essential human virtues; compassion and humanity.

A Poet's Vision

"Sick and Tired of Being Sick and Tired!"

In a riveting speech to the 1964 Democratic National Convention in Atlantic City, Fannie Lou Hamer, Co-Founder and Vice-Chair of the Mississippi Freedom Democratic Party, expressed her frustration with the hypocritical machinations of Democratic party leaders when she declared, "I'm sick and tired of being sick and tired!" A staunch civil rights activist and freedom fighter, she worked with the Student Non-Violent Coordinating Committee (SNCC) to help organize that remarkable "Freedom Summer." Hamer's experience with the deadly virus of white supremacy was up close and extremely personal.

More than fifty years later, we are caught up in the throes of another season of being "sick and tired of being sick and tired!" From the yesterdays of public lynching photographs on the front pages of newspapers to the todays of cell phone videos capturing what some describe as state sanctioned police lynchings. From the Civil Rights era to the Black Lives Matter movement, the current rage is venting the same discontent. From a "good ole boy" President Lyndon Johnson to a narcissistic President Donald Trump, the more things have changed, the more they have remained cruelly the same.

The modern plague of race hatred, racial and political violence will not be stamped out in the United States or in the world until resolute throngs of the "good people" stand up and say, "Enough is enough!" When Donald Trump rallies his support base with the slogan, "Make America Great Again," it reminds many of us that this country's greatness was created in the blast furnace of a social system that for all intents and purposes functioned as an "affirmative action" strategy to enhance the advancement of Americans of European descent.

It took the visceral backlash to an articulate and dignified black man as President and a truly regal black woman as First Lady to make the vicious comedy of Trump's political ascendancy a spiteful reality. Barack Obama could not have been elected to two terms without the support of white people. Then, too many of those same people stumped the pollsters when they voted for Donald Trump. Trump is the same person he has always been. The millions of people who voted for him were not, and are not too bothered by his racism, his misogyny, his crudeness or his lies so long as he serves their self-interest.

The real tragedy in the reactions to the killing of George Floyd, of Breonna Taylor or of Tyre Nichols is no one can claim to have been surprised. The sparks that lit the flames were not new. Newark and Detroit in 1967. Los Angeles in 1992. Ferguson in 2014. Too often, the American conversation on race takes place in a self-serving memory vacuum. These deaths are just emblematic of "the same old same old." Black people are still "Strange Fruit," but this melody is now older than old. Black anger and bitterness have erupted once again because the real truth is Lady Justice is not blind. She has been blindfolded.

In, *Two Nations: Black and White, Separate, Hostile, Unequal,* Andrew Hacker writes, "Race has been an American obsession since the first European sighted 'savages' on these shores. In time, those original inhabitants would be subdued or slaughtered, and finally sequestered out of view. But race took on a deeper and more disturbing meaning with the importation of Africans as slaves…. that Americans of African origin once wore the chains of chattels remains alive in the memory of both races and continues to separate them."

Many Americans ask, "What makes the black experience in America different from other immigrant stories?" First, Africans were kidnapped and transported to the British colonies that became the United States against their will. Designated three fifths of a human being in the original Constitution, the 1857 Dred Scott Supreme Court ruling essentially reaffirmed that black people were not considered citizens. Enslaved Africans were not legally recognized as human beings and as citizens until the ratification of the 13th, 14th and 15th amendments during the 1865-1877 Radical Reconstruction period which expanded the bounds of democracy to include newly freed African Americans.

Their civil rights were then cynically "sold out" to restart the economy when President Rutherford B. Hayes removed federal troops from the south which enabled white southerners to effectively refashion the plantation way of life they lost in war into a Jim Crow peace. The Post-Reconstruction era culminated in the Supreme Court's 1896 Plessy v Ferguson decision that made racial segregation the law of the land. Anti-democratic measures coming out of Republican dominated state legislatures and recent so-called "conservative" Supreme Court rulings signal the mocking resurgence of Jim Crow, renamed, "James," but with the same old face.

The perception of the police as an "occupying force" has been "the everyday" in black communities ever since "paddy rollers" hunted runaways during the slavery times. In America, property values are sacrosanct. This society is spiritually sick. It is time for mainstream America to search its collective heart for answers. If there are "good" police and "sincere" politicians, it is time for them to take a stand against the "bad apples" they KNOW exist within their ranks. We live in a country that is more appalled by the rioters than it is concerned about the combustible conditions that ignited the rioting.

If there is a glimmer of hope in this current reaction to the "disease," it can be found in the diversity of the people that took part in the many peaceful demonstrations. They were black and white. They were Latinx and Asian. They were gay, lesbian, transgender and straight. They represent a generation of young people that has grown up close to each other. Unlike so many of their parents and their grandparents, they do not fear each other. They know each other in ways that were virtually unknown for previous generations.

As they band together, know that we are bearing witness. They are literally beginning to walk the way of a truly New World. They represent another youthful generation challenging their elders and the current group of gridlocked "leaders" to follow their lead.

A Critical Race Reckoning

"Sometimes it seem like to tell the
truth today is to run the risk of being
killed. But if I fall, I'll fall five feet
four inches forward in the fight
for freedom."
>   --Fannie Lou Hamer

The "Big Lie" did not begin with Donald Trump. It began when Europeans emerged from *their* Dark Ages. They set out to explore and to conquer what was, for them, an unknown world. Andrew Hacker provides insight, "Since Europeans first embarked on explorations, they have been bemused by the 'savages' they encountered in new lands. In almost all cases, these 'primitive peoples' were seen as inferior to those who 'discovered' them…the presumption was that these natives could never attain to a stage where they might emulate European achievements."

What twisted logic led Europeans to "discover" places that were already ancient and to define the peoples who discovered *them* when they were lost as primitive savages? The people that encountered Christopher Columbus were driven to near extinction. Now we find them living in remote isolation or brought to life in National Geographic documentaries or preserved in pristine museum exhibits. The real issue is not that so many people believe the so-called "Big Lie," but what is it about the American character that so many people prefer falsehoods in the face of objective, verifiable truth?

Sadly, people often fear what they don't understand, and most Americans don't grasp the disturbing aspects of their history. They know what they have been taught. They believe an America founded as a democracy cannot be a malicious race-based society. They cherish the professed ideals of the Founding Fathers. They simply cannot comprehend the collateral damage caused by the betrayal of those same ideals. All white people are not racist, but will a new generation of activists emerge to confront the pernicious mythology of whiteness Europeans have imposed on the modern world?

If the current discussions about the value of diversity, equity and inclusion are to become meaningful, attention must be focused on the essential worldview that informs Western societies. Inclusion into what? This perilous inter-racial dialogue must be open and honest. It is not enough to only consider the psychological, physical, and spiritual damage that plagues the victims of white supremacy. The Trump vision hearkens back to the America that profited from slavery and Jim Crow—always separate but never equal—racial segregation. He was able to strike the chord of a deep class resentment that has existed in this country for a very long time.

In her groundbreaking but controversial work, *"The Cress Theory of Color Confrontation and Racism (White Supremacy),"* psychiatrist Dr. Frances Cress Welsing contends the *dis-ease* of racism is a potentially treatable mental health condition. Her theory is an earnest attempt to make sense out of observable behavior patterns that have always been senseless. It is on this very level that African Americans and other marginalized peoples of color cannot be expected to put an end to the venomous racial sensibilities that continue to wreak havoc on the quality of our lives.

In this post-George Floyd/Breonna Taylor world, white Americans must finally confront each other about the negative impact of racism in *their* lives. The difficulty of this in-group dialogue notwithstanding, they must face their own personal, as well as their group demons. How did a way of life grounded in the tyranny of skin color identification distort their sense of the true reality of what has always been a multi-racial world? Dr. Welsing writes, "If they are sincere in their attempts to stop the practices of white supremacy (racism) …, whites may be able to find methods to do so once the cause is understood."

This is not about bashing white people. In the same way black people must ask, "What kind of seeds did our ancestors sow such that we, their progeny, reaped dispersal, enslavement and colonization?" Euro-Americans must acknowledge the mess their ancestors left for them to clean up. The human family has always been diverse and the people that describe themselves as white have always been in the numerical minority. However, as conquerors they have fashioned Big Lie after Big Lie. They white-washed their brutality and greed to portray themselves as the arbiters of civilization.

The hijacking of the North American continent, the near extermination of the indigenous peoples, the enslavement of the Africans, the exploitation of their own indentured servant class, and the work-ganging of the Asians have all been recast in the heroic language of democracy building and manifest destiny. It is on this basic level that Americans fear their own historical truths. In America, the truth has always been considered "fake news." They have always preferred "Tall Tales" touting American "exceptionalism."

They have deluded themselves into believing they can ignore the real story and somehow make it go away. They depend on their victims to forgive, to forget, to subsist in stoic suffering and to be thankful we are allowed to live in their presence. They have perfected the art of engaging in what can best be described as "strategic ignorance." They have weaponized their disdain for knowledge into an iron-willed, dangerous concoction of stupidity and arrogance. They see *their* America's downfall everywhere, but especially in "those people." They look for "final" solutions everywhere except in their own hearts.

It is clear, Thomas Jefferson and his fellow Founding Fathers bequeathed their moral quandary, their American dilemma to those future generations that are now struggling under the weight of that heavy load. America has become a society that cannot bear to see itself through the eyes of the human refuse it has created throughout its forced march toward greatness. It is a society that has always refused to look into the mirror to see the reflection of its true face.

I understand some readers will undoubtedly accuse me of contributing to the discord or being "a racist in reverse," while they deny this nation has been divided from the very beginning. America's racial, ethnic, class, religious and lifestyle divisions were established by the Founding Fathers in the face of the human diversity that existed in *their* time.

Jefferson understood they planted poisonous seeds that would one day bear bitter fruit. I suspect he knew that a monstrous debt would have to be paid.

Reading his troubled thoughts in, *Notes on the State of Virginia* (1781), reveals facets of the man they rarely teach in middle and in high school history classes:

"Deep rooted prejudices entertained by the whites; ten thousand recollections, by the blacks, of the injuries they have sustained; new provocations; the real distinctions which nature has made; and many other circumstances will divide us into parties and produce convulsions which will probably never end but in the extermination of the one or the other race."

"I advance it, therefore, as a suspicion only, that the blacks, whether originally a distinct race, or made distinct by time or circumstances, are inferior to the whites in the endowments of both body and mind."

"What a stupendous, what an incomprehensible machine is man! who can endure toil, famine, stripes, imprisonment, or death itself in vindication of his own liberty, and the next moment be deaf to all those motives whose power supported him thro' his trial, and inflict on his fellow men a bondage, one hour of which is fraught with more misery than ages of that which he rose in rebellion to oppose."

Still Strangers

"... most white Americans have been taught to see themselves as individuals, not as members of a privileged group, so they are shaken and angered when blacks deal with them as part of a group, not as individuals. To many whites, this seems a kind of ethical violation. To many blacks, it seems merely realistic. It marks a fundamental difference in perception about the way the world works, with blacks more inclined than whites to recognize the broad forces that determine a group's position in society."

--David K. Shipler

This story is old, but it always presents new plot twists. The Asian communities in the United States are now learning the same lessons that Americans of African descent have known for years. It can be unsafe living in American society. Choosing to be invisible or being tolerated as honorary white people only works until the right buttons are pushed. MAGA President Donald Trump knew how to push those buttons. He unleashed the pent-up white fury that has always existed just below the surface calm.

White supremacy is a spiritual *dis-ease* that continues to prevent this nation from achieving the promise of its lofty rhetoric. The current racial backlash has extended its deadly grasp. Asians—from China, Korea, Viet Nam, Philippines, India, etc.—now find themselves being targeted in ways that must remind WWII generation Japanese Americans of their experiences during that time. Many of their sons were soldiers in the U.S. military when their family property was confiscated and they were forced into detainment campus. Their civil rights were trampled. A new generation is now being jolted out of a false sense of security and finding out they are nothing more than another vulnerable group of non-white "those people."

The specter of race in the United States is always played out inside the drama of black and white. The dangerous life-dance between the people who identify themselves as white and the people *they* designated as black defines the social status of all the other marginalized groups and/or classes of people in relation to mainstream American society. Andrew Hacker asserts, "… members of all these intermediate groups have been allowed to put a visible distance between themselves and Black Americans. Put most simply, none of the presumptions of inferiority associated with Africa and slavery are imposed on these other ethnicities."

He continues, "Moreover, as has been noted, second and subsequent generations of Hispanics and Asians are merging into the 'white' category, partly through intermarriage but also by personal achievement and adaptation. Indeed, the very fact that this is happening sheds light on the tensions and disparities separating the two major races." It seems the dynamics of black life provide the activist template for all of this country's unwanted and rejected. They learn to confront the nature of their oppression when their encounters begin to mirror the African American experience.

Americans find it difficult to reconcile the fact peoples of European descent have imposed their radioactive notions of race and racial differences on a world that has always been racially diverse. They colonized the planet and created empires through the lens of their own distorted self-image. They fabricated an historical narrative that justifies their conquests brandishing the Christian Cross and dresses their aggression in the language of spreading a civilized way of life. The United States was born as a white settler nation out of the global expansion of Europeans outside of Europe.

Hacker offers this telling observation, "Indeed, there is reason to believe that most white Americans still share Thomas Jefferson's belief that in terms of evolution and genetics theirs is the most developed race." This man who carried on a long-term sexual relationship with his slave Sally Hemmings that produced six children, also feared this nation would inevitably fall victim to such sinister ambiguities. Yes, Jefferson was very much a product of his time, but that did not prevent him from recognizing the inherent contradictions in his own behavior.

The mythology of whiteness is so pervasive and has become so embedded in the American way of life that most Americans are simply not conscious of it. They live inside a bubble-reality that appears normal. Conceding that it exists forces them to see themselves in an uncomfortable introspective light. Instead, so many feel smug and superior when Asians or Africans introduce themselves with so-called "Christian" names. They are surprised when people they classify as "aliens" speak "good English." They begrudge the "foreigners" that manage to prosper in spite of the obstacles placed in front of them.

The descendants of the indigenous people that discovered the strange looking creatures at locations the English would rename Jamestown and Plymouth Rock, now call themselves "Indians" and "Native Americans," while living out of sight and out of mind on reservations where they struggle to reclaim cultural identities Americans ruthlessly attempted to eradicate. Although most Americans have no idea of what it means to be the last of one's tribe, the 2017 white supremacist rally in Charlottesville, Virginia revealed the growing numbers of angry young white men who whole heartedly believe the Breitbart/Steve Bannon/Fox News/Tucker Carlson rants about being replaced in a changing America.

The descendants of enslaved Africans live in domestic colonies patrolled by blue uniformed overseers, even as so many of us long to escape from American dreams turned into nightmares. More than 150 years after being declared free with no preparation for freedom, we debate with yet another generation that believes "Nigger" is a proper name. We think money is power and that it holds the key to being free. We are still a people hopelessly damaged by the trauma of believing that good hair/bad hair and light skin/dark skin can somehow define us.

And now, caught up in the "trick bag" of racist stereotypes—they DO NOT all look alike—and their own American Dream aspirations, Asians are waking up to their historical struggle to claim a place in this country where *their* lives matter. Unfortunately, the Supreme Court's ruling on Affirmative Action in college admissions will surely complicate matters because it puts the interests of Asian Americans and African Americans on an avoidable collision course. The changing demographics in 21st century America will require a serious inter-group open channel of communication between so-called peoples of color.

I began this commentary with the quote from David Shipler's, *A Country of Strangers: Blacks and Whites in America,* and I have referenced the insights of Andrew Hacker because I think both writers present a much needed white viewpoint on American race relations. A genuine break through to understanding the origins and the toll of white supremacy on the real quality of life in any society is possible only if enough white people dare to see the negative impact that living in a social system based on "white privilege" has had on their spiritual, emotional, psychological and material development.

If racism is truly a public health crisis, what is that declaration really articulating about the societies the Western world has created? If we are genuinely opposed to those "broad forces that determine a group's position in society," are we not calling out the systems that a ruling class of mostly white men have forged into place? Will this country continue on the destructive path of divisive politricks, denial and willful blindness or will it finally open its eyes to see and open its ears to listen to the chorus of voices crying out from the wilderness?

Yes, white Americans *are* individuals but the fact they have prospered as a group should no longer be open to debate. The racial, ethnic, religious and class divisions that exist in this country only obscure the inevitability that white people will no longer be the majority population in the United States in the not-too-distant future and Spanish will be the most widely spoken language. Are enough Americans willing to view themselves and their society through new insights that incorporate the experiences of those peoples they have traditionally portrayed as non-white?

Undeniably, all lives do matter but there can be no utopian color blindness. An elementary school student once asked, "Why can't people just be like flowers? We don't get mad at a violet because it doesn't look like a rose. All the flowers are beautiful. If everyone looked the same, it would be BORING!" I could only marvel at his pure genius. The innocence of our children can, in fact, guide us. The real question at issue becomes, "Will we follow their lead?" Indeed, there is only one race: the forever beautiful, the forever ugly, the forever diverse human race.

Black Sun in the Western Sky

"Give advice, if people don't listen
let adversity teach them."
    --*Ethiopian proverb*

45 is still circling since being voted out of the White House, but the same "good ole boy" America remains. A more insidious contagion, a spiteful "America First" mentality is still raging. Joe Biden, with Kamala Harris' black presence, has attempted to initiate a healing process, but is recovery possible? Can a nation that has never fully confessed its original sins ever put itself on a path toward healing and reconciliation? Will Americans ever own the near annihilation of the indigenous peoples they claim to have discovered? Can they ever atone for the enslavement of the Africans who were fire burned into a new people inside the white hot crucible of captivity?

Donald Trump cannot be blamed for the consequences wrought by the slave-ocracy the Founding Fathers created; men that betrayed the very principles and values they fought a revolutionary war to protect. 45 was not the first President to deliberately mislead the people. The disturbing revelation is the fact so many people are ready to embrace the deceits and so many politricksters continue to propagate the Trump disinformation. What role did the way this nation projects its self-aggrandizing historical narrative, not only to Americans but to the world, play in the all too predictable attempted insurrection spectacle that played out "all the way live" in the US Capitol on January 6, 2021?

We should not be surprised that Trump's MAGA call resonates so well with his base. Although Abraham Lincoln did begin the process of ending slavery with the Emancipation Proclamation, he also wrote, "There is a physical difference between the white and black race which

I believe will forever forbid the two races living together on terms of social and political equality. And inasmuch as they cannot so live, while they do remain together there must be a position of superior and inferior, and I as much as any other man am in favor of having the superior position assigned to the white race."

The evolution of the Lincoln's racial views can be debated elsewhere, particularly the influence of Frederick Douglas and the Abolitionist movement on his thinking but being distracted by Trump and the extremists that stormed the Capitol diminishes the root causes of the problem. Similar sentiments from Thomas Jefferson, Benjamin Franklin or George Washington can be quoted by those fanatical self-described "patriots" to justify their actions.

Donald Trump's assault on Barack Obama's birth status and his legacy was the signal to "take the country back." The people that attacked the Capitol were not nefarious "Islamic terrorists." They were not F. B. I. branded Black Lives Matter "identity terrorists." They were not Spanish speaking brown hordes over-running the southern border. They were homegrown, Timothy McVay/Oklahoma City/Ruby Ridge/Randy Weaver-like, mostly white Americans.

Trump did not create them. He has always been one of them. Like Mussolini or like Hitler, he was just wickedly shrewd enough to harness and to unleash their pathological fury. This danger has always existed. Racists have always operated throughout the inner workings of this society. They have always been present in all levels of government, in the courts, in the media, in the military, on police forces, in schools, in universities, in churches, in businesses, in healthcare, in sports, in entertainment.

Again, this is not to imply that all white people are racist. They are not. However, the recent and much needed probing exchange of ideas now taking place in response to the madness, although new to some, is not uncovering anything new. The current public discourse is suspect precisely because of its coded and its reactionary character. It leaves many of us reluctant to engage because we are tired of always being cast as "angry" black men and women. Our lack of enthusiasm is rooted in the belief that at this point in American time, too many people have resisted being better informed.

The sweet irony in all of this is the location of the black experience at the matrix of what remains an unfolding drama. From Barack and Michelle Obama as President and First Lady, and now Kamala Harris as Vice-President; from Jimi Hendrix, Marvin Gaye and Whitney Houston transforming the national anthem or Ray Charles singing "God Bless America" with soul; from Muhammad Ali, Tommy Smith and John Carlos taking a stand; from poet laureates Maya Angelou and Amanda Gorman black-poet-treeing inauguration truth to power, the black experience has continuously revealed this nation's unmasked face.

The true measure of the American experiment in democracy continues to be told in the epic story of people of African descent in America. We are not "identity terrorists," but we are a people committed to defining black identities on our own terms. Yes, we are black people, but we are more than the rainbow hues of our skin color. We are a people of African descent, and our ethnic heritage cannot be dismissed, distorted or ignored. Yes, Kamala Harris is part South Asian (India), but her blackness also marks her as a person of African descent (Jamaica).

For a people still searching for a true identity, reducing her to simply being black is to confuse the essential defining points. It is more than ironic that at the same time the country is hailing its first African American/South Asian/female Vice-President, the NFL still remains embroiled in new controversies over team owners continued reluctance to hire black head coaches, despite slick public service announcements designed to placate a predominantly black workforce and to clean up the league's tarnished image. This country has blindly stumbled into another pregnant historical moment.

Martin Luther King lamented, "… I must confess that over the past few years I have been gravely disappointed with the white moderates. I have almost reached the regrettable conclusion that the Negro's great stumbling block in his stride toward freedom is not the white Citizen's Counciler or the Ku Klux Klanner, but the white moderate, who is more devoted to 'order' than to justice; who prefers a negative peace which is the absence of tension to a positive peace which is the presence of justice … who paternalistically believes he can set the timetable for another man's freedom; who lives by a mystical concept of time and who constantly advised the Negro to wait for a 'more convenient season'.…"

African Americans cannot ask others to care about and to respect us more than we care about and respect ourselves. Nigeria's Fela Sowande wrote, "Here in America, a new type of Human Consciousness is being formed and the elements that are going into [it] come from the distilled essences of the various types of Racial-Consciousness in the old world. In this context, the Black American does not merely represent Africa; he is Africa. What the cultured Black American is today, the cultured African must be tomorrow or else become a relic of History. Thus, the Black American is perhaps the most direct link Africa will have with the New World now on the horizon, already casting its shadow on the old."

The Founding Fathers could not have known they were attending to the birth of a truly New World that would evolve far beyond the scope of their Europe-centered imaginations. We are living in a time when all of the world's racial groups are present in *this* society. The days of the United States of America as an exclusive "white man's country" are coming to an end. Is atonement, healing and reconciliation possible? Will we learn to respect each other's story? Will we come to appreciate each other's contributions or will we continue down a path toward blindness and perish in our own foolishness?

Which way will we choose?

When Is Now!

"Until the killing of black men, black mothers' sons, becomes as important to the rest of the country as the killing of a white mother's son, we who believe in freedom cannot rest."

    --Ella Baker

I am a 71-year old black man. I have looked down the barrel of white and black Policemen's guns, each time looking into the fear I could see in *their* eyes. I have been profiled "driving while black." Like my parents before me and their parents before them, my wife and I have had to teach our children, and now our grandchildren, how to make their way in what is still, "the white man's world." We make every effort to convince our children that we have never been the stereotypes portrayed on big and little screens. There will never be a time when black parents will not have to teach our children what it means to be a person of African descent.

Americans only see black people when we serve or entertain them or when we are framed on nightly news broadcasts wreaking havoc in the streets. This nation sees us when we literally leap out of white people's racial nightmares. We are being seen once again, but this time conditions are not the same. Will the nation be able to pay real attention and listen in spite of the noise? As mainstream America wonders why, bankrupt influencers struggle to provide answers beyond the capacity of their surface understanding. Even as they see the realities of black peoples' unbridled fury, too many refuse to concede the deep depths of the heartache that continues to reveal itself.

We are the offspring of ancestors that defied death. This bottomless hurt is centered in people borne of wounded survivors; people that endured the pain of "second class" citizenship under the jack boots of American apartheid. Black voices have always spoken truth to power. Frederick Douglass warned, "Where justice is denied, where poverty is enforced, where ignorance prevails, and where any one class is made to feel that society is an organized conspiracy to oppress, rob and degrade them, neither persons nor property will be safe."

Another generation is burning with an inherited rage. As we watched people set fire to police vehicles and burn down businesses, too few leaders were prepared to admit the degree to which living in impoverished neighborhoods reminds people daily of the conditions this nation is so willing to tolerate. In 1903, W. E. B. DuBois wrote, "The problem of the twentieth century is the problem of the color-line—the relation of the darker to the lighter races of men in Asia and Africa, in America and the islands of the sea."

He forewarned, "Daily the Negro is coming more and more to look upon law and justice, not as protecting safeguards, but as sources of humiliation and oppression. The laws are made by men who have little interest in him; they are executed by men who have absolutely no motive for treating the black people with courtesy or consideration…." MAGA is just a new expression of a mentality that has always existed in this country. It is on this very level that Americans are being forced to confront the affliction ravaging the body politic. This is the deadly predicament the good white people have inherited.

As peaceful demonstrations degenerated into chaos in cities across the country, I wondered if Americans are finally willing to accept how this nation became "great." Yet, hard-fought-for-progress has been achieved. My maternal grandparents escaped a white-hot South Carolina in 1925. My grandmother lived to see three daughters and four grandchildren earn college degrees. I am the son of factory workers who feared for their son who discarded his "slave name." They wondered if I would be able to survive in the white man's world as a proud, uncompromising black poet/professor.

The election of Barack Obama did not signal a "post-racial" phase in America, although my experiences performing before predominantly white audiences as a guest artist with the Cavani String Quartet did allow me to meet genuinely thoughtful white Americans who *do* see.

My poetry provided a glimpse inside a world that was unfamiliar to them. The emergence of MAGA Donald Trump is their generational test. The "I am not racist" Americans are being challenged to *do* something in response to the irrational backlash that is hell-bent on keeping the *Trumpian* vision of America white and right.

How mainstream Americans see black people provides a window into how they prefer to see themselves. These times demand a critical understanding of the psychology of whiteness that has shaped this society and the world. Europeans and peoples of European descent have literally terrorized the planet into submission in the name of civilizing the various peoples of color they determined to be "savages." It is time to lay bare the real nature of the inner desires and secret fears that drive Western societies.

To only focus attention on the more extreme expressions of white supremacy is too convenient. It allows people that benefit from a willfully ignorant white-privilege centered way of life to spurn any responsibility for the destruction inflicted on the decimated communities living just beyond their tranquil suburban neighborhoods, their rural small towns, their urban high rise vistas. The black experience in America is rife with stories that chronicle the inhumanities Americans will disregard to maintain their American dream standard of living. In the last years of his life, Dr. King cautioned, "There is such a time as too late."

People rarely quote the King that admitted, "For twelve years, I, and others like me, had held out radiant promises of progress. I had preached to them about my dream. I had lectured to them about the not too distant day when they would have freedom, 'all here and now.' I had urged them to have faith in America and in white society. Their hopes had soared…. They were booing because we had urged them to have faith in people who had too often proved to be unfaithful. They were now hostile because they were watching the dream that they had so readily accepted turn into a frustrating nightmare."

Instead, King's most famous speech has been co-opted. Michael Eric Dyson writes, "*I Have a Dream*" has been used to chip away at King's enduring social legacy. One phrase has been pinched from King's speech to justify assaults on civil rights in the name of color-blind policies. Moreover, we have frozen King in a timeless mood of optimism that later that very year he grew to question ... we have selectively listened to what King had to say to us that muggy afternoon. It is easier ... to embrace the day's warm memories than to confront the cold realities that led to the March on Washington in the first place. August 28, 1963, was a single moment in time that captured the suffering of centuries. It was an afternoon shaped as much by white brutality and black oppression as by uplifting rhetoric."

Dyson concludes, "Tragically, King's American dream has been seized and distorted by a group of conservative citizens whose forebears and ideology have trampled King's legacy. If King's hope for radical social change is to survive, we must wrest his complex meaning from their harmful embrace. If we are to combat the conservative misappropriation of King's words, we must first understand just how important—and problematic—King's speech has been to American understandings of race for the past thirty years."

For the Trumpians, the goal is a return to an idyllic time that only exists in their minds—a "Gilded Age" when the "Indians" were no more that quaint sounding names and mascots, the "Niggers" were Jim Crowed in plain sight, the "wet backs" were in Mexico, the "slant eyes" were in Asia, the LGBTQ+ crowd was in the closet, the middle and lower class whites knew their places, and women suffered their lives in quiet desperation. The Trump mantra, "My ignorance is greater than your knowledge" is their new standard.

As Black Lives Matter demonstrations took place in London, in Berlin and in other cities around the world, the talking-heads did not reference the King that remarked, "These are revolutionary times. All over the globe men are revolting against old systems of exploitation and oppression, and out of the wounds of a frail world, new systems of justice and equality are being born. The shirtless and barefoot people of the land are rising up as never before. The people who sat in darkness have seen a great light."

The people that condemn the rioting do not invoke the King that sent the following message to Betty Shabazz, the widow of Malcolm X, "... I always had a deep affection for Malcolm and felt that he had a great ability to put his finger on the existence and the root of the problem. He was an eloquent spokesman for his point of view, and no one can honestly doubt that Malcolm had a great concern for the problems we face as a race."

For those who still vilify Malcolm X, they ignore the sentiment he shared with Coretta Scott King just before his assassination in 1965, "I want Dr. King to know that I didn't come to Selma to make his job difficult. I really did come thinking I could make it easier. If the white people realize what the alternative is, perhaps they will be more willing to hear Dr. King." It is time for Americans to understand that Malcolm X and Martin Luther King, Jr. represented opposite sides of the same black coin.

For all the good folk struggling to find answers, if you are ready to listen, the answers you seek have always been there. They are still there. This time around, however, they are revealing themselves in their multi-racial-multi-ethnic-multi-identities glory. Even Thomas Jefferson, in a private moment, wrestled with his troubled conscience when he admitted, "… I tremble for my country when I reflect that God is just; that his justice cannot sleep forever…."

It appears the alternative approach that Malcolm X alluded to may be just beyond the horizon. We must also recognize that there was so much more to the Right Reverend Dr. King than his dream. This slow lurching forward, nevertheless, is not the same as the Civil Rights Movement. The 1960s and the 1970s are behind us. They cannot come back. We can either learn from history or we can be pushed aside by the ever spiraling upward motion of it. I submit that history does not repeat itself. It can and will pass by us in its perpetual process of becoming if we fail to seize our historical moment when it presents itself.

Ella Baker foreshadowed this next phase of the movement we are witnessing being born before our eyes. She argued, "I have always felt it was a handicap for oppressed people to depend so largely upon a leader, because unfortunately in our culture, the charismatic leader usually becomes a leader because *he* (italics mine) has found a spot in the public limelight…. My theory is strong people don't need strong leaders."

The N-Word, or Ashes to Ashes and Dust to Dust

> "The Negro in America must choose between recovering and becoming fully conscious of his own identity or being washed down the plumbless drains of history as a mindless freak of nature."
>
> --Fela Sowande

What historical forces have transpired whereby the descendants of a people that tenaciously clung to being Africans in a strange New World have become a lost people searching for a proper name? What is the connection between what we call ourselves and how we see ourselves? Malcolm X once said, "They called me Nigger so much I thought it was my name." An African proverb teaches, "It is not what you call me, it is what I answer to." I often ask young people, "Do you think a time will ever come when black people stop calling ourselves Niggers?"

I always find it distressing when so many answer with a resounding, "No!" A new generation claims this word today. Many believe if they change the spelling, they can somehow change what it means. It is true that during the slavery period, enslaved Africans transformed this pernicious epithet into a deflective term of endearment. Nevertheless, "Nigger," as concept, is a figment borne of the European/American imagination. Its actual meaning and purpose say more about how white people think of and prefer to see themselves than it can ever really reveal anything about black people as a pejorative target.

The N-word is a feature of the slavery legacy that deserves to be laid to rest annually in elaborate New Orleans-style funeral processions that end with a traditional ritual Burning Ceremony. The extent to which so many African Americans are still transfixed in an almost hypnotic embrace of this classification reflects a condition Dr. Joy DeGruy has identified as, "Post-Traumatic Slave Syndrome." Tragically, we have developed observable pathological behaviors that can be traced back to the slavery era.

Europeans did not bring "slaves" from Africa. They "imported" Africans—Yoruba, Igbo, Mende, Fon, Tikar, Wolof, Mandinka, Akan and more; highly skilled people that did not even describe themselves as "black." They did not get off those slave ships saying, "What's up my Nigga?" They did not know to respond to "Nigger" when they first heard it, but they were conditioned to react to the crack and sting of the whip. When they answered to it, they did not get hit. Slave masters renamed their "slaves" precisely because they recognized the importance of traditional African names.

Enslaved Africans knew their names. They understood themselves in direct relation to the sense of identity and cultural heritage safeguarded in their names. It is now possible to study the behavior modification process of turning Africans into "slaves." To be sure, I grew up using the N-word. My friends used it. My parents used it. "Nigger" resounded all around us all the time. I did not know, then, that we did not know better. Rather than rail against its rampant use in today's pop culture, we need to focus more attention on why the entertainment industry has such a compelling and vested interest in keeping it alive?

When I learned the real story of the African experience in the Americas, it made it possible to *overstand* these horrible chapters from the book of the black past. Walking through what are no longer Doors of No Return at slaving forts in West Africa moved me to rethink the terms we use to describe ourselves. At Assin Manso in Ghana, where captured Africans were given their "Last Bath" after being force-marched to the coast, the tour guide quoted Kwame Nkrumah, "We are not Africans because we are born in Africa, we are Africans because Africa is born in us." A people ignorant of their origins is a people susceptible to being defined and controlled.

The persistent use of the N-word speaks to the obscene nature of our mental enslavement. But *overstanding* is precious. We are a suffering people still. Frederick Douglass cautioned, "Find out just what any people will quietly submit to, and you have the exact measure of the injustice and wrong which will be imposed on them." Are we the "Niggers" that so many enslaved Africans were "seasoned" into being, or will we rediscover and finally become the original human beings we were born into this world to be? We are descended from ancestors who dared to dream that one day we would truly be free.

The Way Forward

> Healing is work, not gambling. It is the work of inspiration, not manipulation…. The work of healing is work for inspirers working long and steadily in a group that grows over generations, until there are inspirers, healers wherever our people are scattered, able to bring us together again.
>
> --*Ayi Kwei Armah*

If we are to become a whole people once again, both collective as well as individual healing must take place. Too many psychic wounds remain open and festering. This generation to generation pain is too real. Although some things have changed, far too many are worse than the same. We are a people held captive for so long, we no longer have memories of having once been "free." Somehow, we survive. We continue to find ways to thrive in spite of new, more insidious means to prevent black people from turning "promise land" dreams into new realities.

Colin Kaepernick belongs to a long line of determined voices that have called out the naked power of American society. As soon as enslaved Africans learned to command the languages of their enslavers, a complicated inter-racial-life-and-death-dance-dialogue began in earnest. In this country, black folk cried out in wailing sorrow songs, "Sometimes I feel like a motherless child, a long way from home," and survived with cunning Brer Rabbit "mother wit." This self-determination is still there in the "gut bucket" resilience that echoes inside the music that continues to guide us around and through the hurt.

The systematic rape of Africa fueled the Trans-Atlantic "slave" trading era. Walter Rodney writes, "In the centuries before colonial rule, Europe increased its economic capacity by leaps and bounds, while

Africa appeared to have been almost static…. The relevant fact is that what was a slight difference when the Portuguese sailed to West Africa in 1444 was a huge gap by the time European robber statesman sat down in Berlin 440 years later to decide who should steal which parts of Africa…. which provided … the opportunity for Europe to move into the imperialist epoch … and further under develop Africa."

If there is going to be a genuine discussion of "systemic racism" in this society, a proper historical back ground must be established. The United States has always been a nation hopelessly trapped between two powerful opposing forces: the projected illusion, "Land of the free and home of the brave" vs the actual aristocratic American Slaveocracy. The lives of indigenous peoples never-mattered. Black lives never mattered. Indentured servant lives never really mattered. Women, no matter their color or class, only mattered as prized possessions.

Black folk have always spoken out. Olaudah Equiano wrote, "When you make men slaves you deprive them of half their virtue, you set them, in your own conduct, an example of fraud, rapine, and cruelty, and compel them to live with you in a state of war." He knew the natural enemy of the slave is his master and the natural enemy of the master is his slave. Frederick Douglass understood, "It is not the light we need, but fire; it is not the gentle shower, but thunder. We need the storm, the whirlwind, and the earthquake."

Since the murder of George Floyd, the fire, the thunder, the storm, the whirlwind and the earthquake have all occurred. To simply showcase black and brown faces in highly visible positions is not the remedy to cure the illness that is a blight in any white society, especially when those darker faces merely become facades disguising the same forces of white supremacy. Just as some African "Royals" were complicit in the selling of Africans into slavery, there are self-serving black leaders, today, that oblige the interests of the power brokers that continue to undermine black lives.

I began this offering with an excerpt from, *The Healers*, by Ghana's Ayi Kwei Armah, because I identify with the story and its main characters. When Master Healer Damfo tells Densu, "The present is where we get lost—if we forget our past and have no vision of the future…," his message resonates even more at this momentous point we are experiencing in *this* "Eternal Now" time. The United States is a land in desperate need of spiritual healing. The *dis-ease* of white supremacy is a malignancy devouring its collective soul. Black people living in this country have been indelibly scarred by this scourge.

If this nation is to ever become the society it professes to be on paper, white people must confront their own personal, as well as their group insecurities. Dr. Frances Cress Welsing diagnosed racism as a potentially treatable mental illness in her controversial work, *The Cress Theory of Color Confrontation and Racism (White Supremacy): A Psychogenetic Theory and World Outlook*. Whether her theory is plausible is not really the point. It is an earnest attempt to make sense out of observable behavior patterns that have always been senseless.

She writes, "... [the] white peoples of the world presumably also could benefit from such an awareness of the motivation behind behaviors that often baffle them. If they are sincere in their attempts to stop the practices of white supremacy (racism), whites may be able to find methods to do so once the cause is understood. Perhaps some psychiatrist will develop a method of mass psychotherapy (i. e. therapeutic counter-racist theater) to help whites become comfortable with their color and their numbers. However, one can foresee a major problem arising from the possible difficulty of motivating whites to release the secondary gains historically derived from the racist system."

Second, they must accept the legitimacy of diverse multi-cultural voices. Americans must listen to the stories of the not-European experience in what they call the New World as told by those people they classify as non-white. When black people do speak to what we see and what we know, white people invariably go on the defensive. They dismiss or deflect a perspective that requires a level of self-awareness which can be unsettling. Many white people tend to operate from the belief that their perception of reality *is* the reality. They unconsciously and often consciously resist the possibility that valid alternative perspectives do exist.

Third, black people in America must begin to understand that we are an essential part of a global community of Africans and peoples of African descent. We must finally embrace our own diversity. We have evolved into new tribes. African Americans are one of several distinct peoples of African descent—i. e. Jamaicans, Afro-Cubans, Afro-Brazilians, Haitians, etc.—that emerged in the Americas. We are a people of many hues, body types, skin tones and hair textures. Given the sexual dynamics of life in the New World, we must make peace with having become a multi-racial people.

African Americans are urban, suburban and rural. We are Democrats, Republicans, Independents, while some of us have never believed in nor participated in the "politricks" of a "shitstem" that has always been corrupt. We are Christians. We are Muslims. Rastas. Hebrews. Buddhists. Agnostics. We practice traditional African ways of life and more. We have family members who belong to the diverse LGBTQ+ communities. We must learn how to respect, how to protect, how to value, how to love, and how to genuinely communicate with each other.

We must rediscover how to connect with the true essence of our heritage as an African derived people—the good, the bad, the ugly. Self-knowledge is the key to navigating life in white society. It was not until I stood in the open Door of No Return in the House of Slaves on Senegal's Goree Island that first time did being born African in America begin to make sense to me. I was able to lay this heavy burden down. It took a pilgrimage to ancestral lands to begin to put the fragments of my Self back together. This nation does need spiritual healing, but I am more concerned with engaging the intragroup discourse black people so desperately need to have with each other.

A black agenda can never be dependent upon who occupies whatever corporate, academic or elected office—including the White House. This does not mean people in those positions do not have roles to play but operating inside this system does not lend itself to doing the necessary work needed to reclaim our communities. In too many ways, we have become more American than the Americans. We have become victims of the same hard-headedness. We suffer from the same social sclerosis. Healing is possible, but we must stop ignoring the signs and only if we stop wallowing in the "rugged individualism" that is crippling this society.

The daunting work of putting shattered black lives back together is a formidable undertaking. I have even heard it suggested, "If we are to save ourselves from white people, we will have to help save them from themselves." An intriguing proposition indeed, but I think we will have to debate its merits in conference amongst ourselves. Do we accept the mistaken notion the black experience begins with slavery in the United States or do we recognize the Afrocentric view that it begins in Africa and this exile in the New World merely represents chapters in an epic saga that is still unfolding?

If we do not work to save ourselves, who will save us? We cannot turn away from this work because it will not be completed in this life time. Early in the 20th century, black activists declared the birth of a "New Negro Renaissance" in Harlem. Africa's lost tribes were awakening from the Dark Ages of Enslavement and Colonialism. The movement ebbs and flows but it never stops. Previous generations struggled to break out of the chains that restricted black bodies. Hopefully the coming generations will continue the quest to break the fetters that still shackle black minds.

We should heed Master Healer Damfo's final lesson to Densu as life-giving wisdom from the ancestors, "Often, our confusion comes merely from impatience. The disease has run unchecked through centuries. Yet sometimes we dream of ending it in our little lifetimes, and despair seizes us if we do not see the end in sight. A healer needs to see beyond the present and tomorrow. He needs to see years and decades ahead. Because healers work for results so firm, they may not be wholly visible till centuries have flowed into millennia. Those willing to do this necessary work, they are the healers of our people."

Race: The Elephant in the Room

> "There is a cult of ignorance in the United States, and there has always been. The strain of anti-intellectualism has been a constant thread winding its way through our political and cultural life, nurtured by the false notion that democracy means that 'my ignorance is just as good as your knowledge.'"
>
> --Isaac Asimove

The weaponization of ignorance and arrogance are the real dangers in these treacherous yet exciting times. The misguided battle over Critical Race Theory (CRT) being taught in schools, the attack on African American history in Florida, in Arkansas; the legislative assault on "… colleges being too woke," on notions of Diversity, Equity, and Inclusion (DEI), and on the fundamentals of academic freedom here in Ohio are being waged to conserve an archaic status quo that was never intended to embrace 21st century American lives.

Most of the mean spirited combatants introducing racist, homophobic, and misogynistic legislation at all levels of government or the moblike "parents" showing up and disrupting school board meetings are making their intentions clear. They want to rename Jim Crow, "James," as if we would not recognize him dressed in a new suit of clothes. It is beyond their myopic tunnel vision to recognize the cynical ways they have been duped into becoming disposable pawns in a sinister grifter's game. That so many mostly white Americans actually believe Trump-like leaders are their champions is the real "head scratcher." Nevertheless, what is routinely described as a "culture war" is not new.

This mortal combat has been joined to regain control of an historical narrative in which untruths were transformed into a vainglorious national mythology. The critical question in dispute: "Did the Founding Fathers establish the "world's greatest" Democracy, or did they effectively create a sophisticated *Slave-ocracy* sustained by a political economy constructed on the foundation of chattel slavery? This conflict is about reestablishing who has the power to define and how that power will be used to characterize a changing 21st century America.

How a story is told, and from whose point of view the story is told, often determines what that story will mean to those who hear and accept it. The Founding Fathers never imagined the demographic changes that now characterize an ever-evolving United States or how these changes are challenging old notions that are not capable of incorporating a present-day American landscape. The legend of the United States as a cultural "Melting Pot" has never really been viable.

The new gate keepers are calling for the banning of books under the guise of protecting young people. They fear their children will somehow be traumatized if they learn how European "conquerors" burned indigenous manuscripts, desecrated sacred artifacts, ransacked pre-American societies that were already ancient, enslaved Africans, exploited their own indentured servants and conscripted Asians into work gangs, not only to make America great but to improve the standard of living of Europeans and peoples of European descent.

The domain of education remains the primary battleground where the war to control the cherished American narrative is being waged. This struggle has always been about grouping the stories of indigenous people, of people of African descent, and of other non-white people within the framework of a competitive class based social system of white preferment. The present Black Lives Matter awakening can be traced to three notable developments in a movement that actually began when the first Africans were traded for supplies at the Jamestown settlement in 1619.

Carter G. Woodson's 1933 publication, *The Mis-Education of the Negro,* the 1954 Brown v Board of Ed decision that struck down racial segregation in the schools, and the 1960s/1970s black student led Black Studies revolt that challenged the core tenets of American education are pivotal. The sanctity of the accepted storyline is under threat and educators find themselves trapped in between antagonistic forces. One side committed to the status quo and defiantly resistant to change, the other side just as doggedly determined to claim inclusion in a system that can no longer remain exclusively patriarchal and Euro-centric.

Woodson argued, "… the educational system as it has developed both in Europe and America is an antiquated process which does not hit the mark even in the case of the needs of the white man himself. If the white man wants to hold on to it, let him do so; but the Negro, so far as he is able, should develop and carry out a program of his own." Efforts to establish independent black educational initiatives and institutions are not new. Some contend they are needed now more than ever.

He wrote, "… the philosophy and ethics resulting from our educational system have justified slavery, peonage, segregation, and lynching. The oppressor has the right to exploit, to handicap, and to kill the oppressed. Negroes daily educated in the tenets of such a religion of the strong have accepted the status of the weak as divinely ordained, and during the last three generations of their nominal freedom they have done practically nothing to change it. Their pouting and resolutions indulged in by a few of the race have been of little avail."

Woodson asserted, "… taught the same economics, history, philosophy, literature and religion which have established the present code of morals, the Negro's mind has been brought under the control of his oppressor. The problem of holding the Negro down, therefore, is easily solved. When you control a man's thinking you do not have to worry about his actions." The Brown ruling galvanized the Civil Rights/Black Power Movement. It focused attention on the physical, psychological, emotional, and spiritual devastation being ensnared in white society has rained down on black people and especially on black youth.

According to Dr. Joy DeGruy, "P.T.S.S. (Post-Traumatic Slave Syndrome) is a theory that explains the etiology of many of the adaptive survival behaviors in African American communities throughout the United States and the Diaspora. It is a condition that exists as a consequence of the multigenerational oppression of Africans and their descendants resulting from centuries of chattel slavery. A form of slavery which was predicated on the belief that African Americans were Inherently/genetically inferior to whites. This was then followed by institutionalized racism which continues to perpetuate injury."

The Kyle Rittenhouse acquittal, the empty gesture of censuring Rep. Paul Gosar and Texas Gov. Greg Abbott's promise to pardon convicted murderer Daniel Perry merely reaffirms that black lives do not matter and white lives that confront the system in support of black lives do not matter. America is as America does. The very public outrage in response to CRT or the hollow retort of "all lives matter" in reaction to Black Lives Matter protests corroborates a stubborn white America's refusal to acknowledge the real consequences of the twin legacies of slavery and Jim Crow racial segregation.

Europeans and peoples of European descent have bullied the planet in the name of spreading the alleged benefits of Western civilization. The peoples descended from the conquered, the enslaved and the colonized are now derisively referred to as the "Third World." To admit that black people and other so-called peoples of color have a legitimate right to be aggrieved and to demand reparations requires a collective look inward that too many Americans cannot bear to indulge. It is on this level that the Black Studies Movement has been in the vanguard of the effort to renew American education for more than 50 years.

In *Out of the Revolution: The Development of Africana Studies,* Delores P. Aldridge and Carlene Young state, "The systematic study of the African American experience from its African heritage to contemporary society and beyond is nowhere else pursued in the academy than in Black Studies programs. Although the body of knowledge … has been available to scholars for several generations, it was not until the black consciousness movement of the 1960s forced the issue that African Americans began to be accorded their rightful place in the annals of the history and development of American society. The security of that progress depends on the existence of Black Studies programs."

As a professor of Black Studies for more than 40 years, I can testify to the transformative impact this discipline has had on all students—black, white or otherwise. From the 19th century Underground Railroad through the Radical Reconstruction era to the early 20th century

Harlem Renaissance/New Negro/Marcus Garvey Movement through the mid-20th century Black Consciousness/Black Arts Movement to the current millennial Hip Hop inspired Black Lives Matter challenge, the struggles of African Americans have provided the model for other marginalized groups to claim their rightful places in American society.

The conflict over CRT is typical subterfuge. Martin Luther King, Jr. articulated the real issue when he wrote, "Whites, it must frankly be said, are not putting in a similar mass effort to re-educate themselves out of their racial ignorance. It is an aspect of their superiority that the white people of America believe they have so little to learn. The reality of substantial investment to assist Negroes into the twentieth century, adjusting to Negro neighbors and genuine school integration is still a nightmare for all too many white Americans."

The opposition to CRT, to Black Studies, Women's Studies, Latinx Studies, LGBTQ+ Studies, and to DEI initiatives are fundamentally the same. Not all, but too many "older" white Americans dread the idea of giving critical thinking tools to young people that would empower them to not only challenge their elders and the status quo but to also reject the inherent advantages of white privilege. Matters of race continue to be the proverbial elephant in the room.

Who can deny that this nation is engaged in a classic struggle to influence not just how, but who will create *the* authentic anthology of the diverse and inclusive American stories that must be celebrated, that must finally be told?

Invented Reality: Trump/DeSantis/Republican Insanities

"Racists will always call you a racist when you identify their racism. To love yourself now is a form of racism. We are the only people who are criticized for loving ourselves, and white people think when you love yourself you hate them. No, when I love myself they become irrelevant to me."
    --Dr. John Henrik Clarke

How many more lives will Donald A. Trump ruin before his enthralled "deaf, dumb and blind" base finally realizes that he and his fawning Republican sycophants have never really cared for or about them? From the Taj Mahal Casino Atlantic City debacle or the Central Park 5 or Charlottesville or the failed January 6th insurrection or MAGA President Donald Trump to Anti-Disney, the Anti-LGBTQ+, the Anti-African American history, the Anti-Wokism, the self-proclaimed "Guardian of the Narrative" Ron DeSantis, the political heirs to the people Richard Nixon once dubbed, "the silent majority," are determined to invent their own reality. They will call it "historical truth," and move to impose their warped vision on the larger society in the name of *their* distorted "American values."

The real point at issue remains, "Why are so many Americans so willing to believe in big lies?" The actual "false narrative" began when the Founding Fathers established the original Big Lie. Dr. John Henrik Clarke adds, "Europeans not only colonized most of the world, but they also colonized information about the world." That Europeans—including a fledgling United States—engaged in the Trans-Atlantic slave trade for more than three centuries is no false narrative. That certain members of African royalty were complicit in collaborating with the Europeans is no false narrative. That several American Presidents—most notably George Washington and Thomas Jefferson—were slave owners is no false narrative.

Florida Governor Ron DeSantis is a graduate of Yale and Harvard Universities. One wonders if he learned what he believes to be the fundamentals of African American history at those institutions, even though both are home to prestigious African American Studies Departments. The University of Florida and Florida State University have African American Studies Programs. Florida International University has an African American and Diaspora Studies Program. The state of Florida is also home to five HBCUs—including Florida A & M and Bethune-Cookman.

So-called distinguished scholars have always provided the rationale to support and to justify the false assumptions of white supremacy. Leslie A. Fiedler wrote, "… but the Negro arrived [in the U.S.] without a past, out of nowhere; that is to say, out of a world he is afraid to remember [and], perhaps could not even formulate to himself in the language he has been forced to learn. Before America, there is for him simply nothing." Hugh Trevor-Roper, wrote, "Undergraduates, seduced as always, by the changing breath of journalistic fashion, demand that they should be taught African history. Perhaps in the future there will be some African history to teach. But at present there is none: there is only the history of Europeans in Africa. The rest is darkness….. and darkness is not a subject of history."

If Africa truly had no history or culture, why are so many European museums filled with priceless African artifacts? If enslaved Africans were, indeed, "savages" with no skills, they would have been of no practical use to European or American plantation owners. Yoruba artisans were already working with metals—iron and bronze. They did not need Europeans to "teach" them how to become blacksmiths. Europeans had no agricultural traditions in growing cotton or rice or sugar cane. They could not teach skills to enslaved Africans those Africans had already mastered.

Yoruba farmers were already cultivating cotton. Mende farmers were already cultivating rice. Hausa people were already master horsemen. Ashanti and Mandinka peoples were already mining gold, which convinced Europeans to refer to West Africa as the "Gold Coast." Storytellers, singers, dancers and players of instruments were already keepers of the way of life. Traditional Priests and Healers were already guardians of an African worldview that encompassed a dynamic relationship to the creation of the universe and their place in it. African people were kidnapped and targeted for slavery precisely because of the skills they possessed.

That the English built the male slave dungeons at Cape Coast beneath their Anglican Church or the Portuguese converted the Confessional and Sanctuary into an auction site at their Catholic Church in Elmina is no false narrative. The English Founding Fathers reduced enslaved Africans to chattel and codified them as three fifths of a human being in the original Constitution. The DeSantis insanity is really about who will define and control the "accepted" American story. It is about rolling back the real hard-fought-for-progress that African Americans, women and other marginalized groups have achieved over the last several decades.

DeSantis speaks of protecting the American narrative. It is evident he has not thoroughly read Jefferson or Benjamin Franklin's *Observations Concerning the Increase of Mankind* (1751). He does not want students exposed to the wisdom of enslaved African Americans. Harriet Tubman maintained, "I've heard 'Uncle Tom's Cabin' read, and I tell you Mrs. Stowe's pen hasn't begun to paint what slavery is as I have seen it at the far South. I've seen de real thing, and I don't want to see it on no stage or in no theater." Frederick Douglass argued, "Men talk of the Negro problem. There is no Negro problem. The problem is whether the American people have honesty enough, loyalty enough, honor enough, patriotism enough to live up to their Constitution."

Donald A. Trump is *the* self-anointed leader of a MAGA crusade that is more cult than movement. Shamelessly anti-democratic Ron DeSantis is determined to out-Trump Trump. Extremist Republicans have willingly embraced becoming the new face of fascism in the United States. It can be argued that many Americans do not really grasp how their democracy is designed to work. It is revealing that a society which claims to be, "One Nation Under God," routinely devolves into factions railing against "outsiders" or "outside agitators" whenever their fellow Americans speak out against injustice no matter the state.

Too many Americans who genuinely celebrate their own revolutionary Founding Fathers, hypocritically label any views they disagree with as "socialist," as "radical left," as "extremist" and as "dangerous." They forget the Founding Fathers were considered "insurrectionists." They conveniently forget George Washington would have been executed for treason had he been captured by the British. They have no shame. They have no decency. They know we know. They do not care. Real life truth in the United States is harsh. America's "experiment in Democracy" is on trial and the whole world is watching.

Big Lies

"A system cannot fail those it was never meant to protect."
        --W. E. B. DuBois

The malevolence that Europeans brought with them when they were lost yet claimed to discover a "New World" that was already ancient is putrefying in this society. The "Big Lie" began when they hijacked this hemisphere under the banner of "God, Gold, and Glory." American lies metastasized when the English Founding Fathers eloquently proclaimed a Democracy based on the principle that "all men are created equal," while they proceeded to fashion a class-based society grounded in the philosophy of white supremacy.

The Founders launched this nation for white men who owned property in particular and for white people in general. They debated with each other and then executed treacherous, life altering decisions that decimated the peoples they viewed as standing in the way of their progress. Eight American presidents were slave owners during their tenures in office. They knew slavery was evil, but they valued power, property, and profits more. Thomas Jefferson admitted, "I tremble for my country when I reflect that God is just; that his justice cannot sleep forever...."

Poisonous beliefs on race, class and gender have always been the glaring flaws securely embedded in the foundation of the American Republic. Benjamin Franklin believed in acknowledging his life's failings; what he called, his "Errata." A former slave owner, nearing the end of his life, he accepted the Presidency of the Pennsylvania Society Promoting the Abolition of Slavery. He appealed to both houses of Congress to consider the hypocrisy of the existence of slavery in the face of their newly ratified Constitution. He understood the full implications for a fledgling United States of America's "experiment in democracy."

In an 1824 letter to Lydia Huntley Sigourney, Thomas Jefferson wrote, "I rejoice also in your advocation for the Indians rights and concur in all your sentiments in their favor.... I wish that was the only blot in our moral history, and that no other race had higher charges to bring against us. I am not apt to despair; yet I see not how we are to disengage ourselves from that deplorable entanglement, we have the wolf by the ears and feel the danger of either holding or letting him loose. I shall not live to see it but those who come after us will be wiser than we are, for light is spreading and man improving. To that advancement I look, and to the dispensations of an all-wise and all-powerful providence to devise the means of effecting what is right."

Americans have been misled for so long, the historical lies have become the twisted hallowed truth. Recent Supreme Court decisions reversing precedents in abortion rights and affirmative action make it abundantly clear that too many leaders in today's America are dangerously far from being "wiser." This was not the first time the Supreme Court has reversed itself. The 1896 Plessy and the 1954 Brown rulings speak to the "which way are the political and social winds blowing" nature of historic land mark court decisions.

The Founding Fathers were imperfect men that were blinded by the bright white light of their own glittering contradictions. They were predominantly landowners who glorified their whiteness in the theology of a jealous, vengeful God. They conducted genocidal wars against the native inhabitants they claim to have "discovered" and carved out a nation in a strange New World. They reduced Africans to legal "beasts of burden" and codified a people as chattel. They rationalized the ruthless exploitation of the indentured servant classes. They designated all women as one of their more precious and prized possessions.

It is painfully clear the Divine providence Jefferson envisioned is not shining very brightly on this nation today. Even as the January 6th Committee detailed the depths of former President Donald Trump's brazen attempt to overturn the 2020 Presidential election results, Republican sycophants have been elected to office trumpeting the same lies. Trump's MAGA world longs to return to a Puritanical past when a fanatical minority could impose its will on all the people according to their warped interpretation of American values.

They want to put women back in their "proper" place—seen, not heard, without voice, barefoot, pregnant, without power. The peoples of the *First Nations* must remain out of sight and out of mind on desolate reservations. It means keeping the descendants of enslaved Africans in check—invisible but hidden in plain view. It involves perverting the 2nd amendment to fabricate a rationale making it easier to put more guns into more hands in response to more Charlestons, more Sandy Hooks, more Parklands, more Pittsburghs, more El Pasos, more Buffalos, more Uvaldes and more Colorado Springs.

That our contemporary understanding of the Constitution should be tempered by what we think the Founding Fathers "meant" when they crafted it in their time *is* the problem. Their narrow 18th century worldview does not fit this society's 21st century multi-racial, multi-ethnic, multi-religious and diverse lifestyle reality. It remains to be seen if another generation of shocked Americans are outraged enough to finally compel their political, their religious, their educational and their civic leaders to "devise the means of effecting what is right."

Whether America is willing to change its hate-filled ways or not is entirely in the hands of those "good" people that truly believe in its lofty rhetoric. The world is changing and peoples of color are determined to reclaim control over our destinies. We cannot become sidetracked by the monstrous predicament the Western world has inherited from their forebearers. Today, the great American Ship-of-State is reeling in the hands of mean-spirited *politricksters* playing perilous power games with " We the People's" lives. America can either evolve in harmony with a transforming world or be rendered irrelevant by it.

When I was a young poet, after sharing a poem to introduce Maya Angelou, she pulled me aside later that evening and cautioned, "Bitterness gives nothing back." I did not understand, then, how she was trying to get me to see that hating white people can never be a solution. It would only intensify our own self-hatred. Hating them would only confirm that we have succumbed to the same *dis-ease*. It would signal that we have fallen prey to the very thing we despise. We can either step back and seek a healing antidote or we can be forever consumed by it.

Black people cannot resolve the fears, the inner desires or the insecurities that white people must confront in themselves. We must face up to our own fears, inner desires and insecurities. If Chief Fela Sowande's vision of "a new type of Human Consciousness ... being formed and the elements that are going into [it] come from the distilled essences of the various types of Racial-Consciousness in the old world," is, indeed, evolving here in United States, then embracing and appreciating the Black, Brown, Red, Yellow, and White diversity of the human family is the only sane, humane way forward.

Who can say if Americans will ever genuinely appreciate the gifts black people have contributed to the making of the United States? Who can say if America will ever fulfil its promise? Our enslaved ancestors sang, "This little light of mine, I'm gonna make it shine," and they brought Black light into this White dark world. In spite of the roadblocks and the set-backs, I believe we *can* restore balance and harmony in black life, but only if we can reclaim the mighty power that has always been present in black hands. If we can heal ourselves, perhaps it might provide a pathway for this troubled nation to find redemption and to heal its collective Self.

Epilogue

"Every great dream begins with a dreamer. Always remember, you have within you the strength, the patience and the passion to reach for the stars to change the world."

--Harriet Tubman

Suggested Reading

Out of the Revolution: The Development of Africana Studies, Delores P. Aldridge and Carlene Young

2000 Seasons, Ayi Kwei Armah

The Healers, Ayi Kwei Armah

By Any Means Necessary

Malcolm X: Real, Not Reinvented, Edited by Herb Boyd, Ron Daniels, Maulana Karenga and Haki R. Madhubuti

Post Traumatic Slave Syndrome, Joy DeGruy

The Souls of Black Folk, W. E. B. DuBois

Two Nations: Black and White, Separate, Hostile, Unequal, Andrew Hacker

Stamped From The Beginning: The Definitive History of Racist Ideas in America, Ibram X. Kendi

Where Do We Go from Here: Chaos or Community?, Martin Luther King, Jr.

Malcolm X: A Life of Reinvention, Manning Marable

How Europe Under-Developed Africa, Walter Rodney

A Country of Strangers: Blacks and Whites in America, David K. Shipler

The Healing Wisdom of Africa, Malidoma Patrice Some

The Spirit of Intimacy, Sobonfu Some

The Isis Papers: The Keys to the Colors, Frances Cress Welsing

The Mis-Education of the Negro, Carter G. Woodson

About the Author

Born Wilbur Thomas Smith, Jr. in Orange but raised in Vaux Hall, New Jersey, **Mwatabu S. Okantah** holds the BA in English and African Studies from Kent State University (1976) and the M.A. in Creative Writing from the City College of New York (1982). A Professor and Chair in the Department of Africana Studies at Kent State University, he also serves as Director of the Ghana Study Abroad Program. He has taught at Union College, The Livingston College of Rutgers University, Cleveland State University and Lakeland Community College.

Okantah is the author of *Guerrilla Dread: Poetry for the Heart and Minds* (2019), *Cheikh Anta Diop: Poem for the Living*—a limited trilingual edition in English, French and Wolof (2017/1997), *Muntu Kuntu Energy: New and Selected Poetry* (2013), *Reconnecting Memories: Dreams No Longer Deferred* (2004), *Legacy: for Martin and Malcolm* (1987), *Collage* (1984) and *Afreeka Brass* (1983). Work has been anthologized in *A Poem Demic* (2022), *Speak A Powerful Magic* (2019), *In the Company of Russell Atkins* (2016), *Gwendolyn Brooks and Working Writers* (2007), *Beyond the Frontier: African American Poetry for the 21st Century* (2002), *The Second Set, Vol. II* (1996) and *Soul Looks Back in Wonder* (1994). A new work, *The View from Stono: Reflections, Reminiscences and Ruminations,* is forthcoming.

Honors include the 2021 Alice Dunbar Nelson Literary Achievement Award, a 2019 BMe Genius Fellowship ($10,000), a 2019 Albert Nelson Marquis Lifetime Achievement Award and a 1988 Rotary International Group Study Fellowship to Nigeria. He has performed as **Griot** for the **Iroko African Drum & Dance Society** and as a **Guest Artist** with **Vince Robinson and the Jazz Poets** and with the **Cavani String Quartet**. When called upon, he still throws down with his own **Muntu Kuntu Energy Ensemble**.

He lives in Kent, Ohio with his wife, Aminah.
www.mkepoet1.com